TUDOR REBELLIONS

Table of Contents

Bigod's Rebellion	1
Cornish Rebellion of 1497	2
Desmond Rebellions	4
Exeter Conspiracy	6
Jack of the North	7
Kett's Rebellion	7
List of Tudor Rebellions	12
Oxfordshire Rising of 1596	12
Pilgrimage of Grace	14
Prayer Book Rebellion	15
Ridolfi plot	19
Rising of the North	20
Second Cornish Uprising of 1497	21
Stafford and Lovell Rebellion	22
The Earl of Essex Rebellion	22
Wyatt's rebellion	22

Preface

Each chapter in this book ends with a URL to a hyperlinked online version. Use the online version to access related pages, websites, footnotes, tables, color photos, updates, or to see the chapter's contributors. Click the edit link to suggest changes. Please type the URL exactly as it appears. If you change the URL's capitalization, for example, it may not work.

Purchase of this book entitles you to a free trial membership in the publisher's book club at www.booksllc.net. (Time limited offer.) Simply enter the barcode number from the back cover onto the membership form on our home page. The book club entitles you to select from millions of books at no additional charge, including a PDF copy of this and related books to read on the go. Simply enter the title or subject onto the search form to find them.

If you have any questions, could you please be so kind as to consult our Frequently Asked Questions page at www.booksllc.net/faqs.cfm? You are also welcome to contact us there.

Publisher: Books LLC, Wiki Series, Memphis, TN, USA, 2013.

Bigod's Rebellion

Bigod's Rebellion of January 1537 was an armed rebellion by English Roman Catholics in Cumberland and Westmorland against King Henry VIII of England and the English Parliament. It was led by Sir Francis Bigod, of Settrington in the North Riding of Yorkshire.

Following the Pilgrimage of Grace of 1536, the King had made promises which had not been kept and, in January 1537, a new rising began to take shape, although Robert Aske (a leader of the Pilgrimage of Grace) tried to prevent it.

An undated letter from Aske to the Commons, probably early in 1537, tells them: "Neighbours, I do much [marvel] that ye would assemble yourselves with Bigod [seeing how] earnestly the King's highness extendeth general pardon to all this North". He goes on that the king intends to hold a parliament at York and to have the new Queen crowned. Bigod had intended to destroy the effect of previous petitions, but "as I hear you were forced to assemble by his threats and menaces, I shall declare this to the King, and fear not but that you shall have his Grace's pardon notwithstanding".

Lord Darcy wrote to Aske and Robert Constable on 17 January Of Sir Fras. Bigod I heard, this day at dinner, as you wrote; and more, that Hallum was taken at Hull yesterday with a letter in his purse from Sir Francis Bigod promising that he and all the West Countries would rise and come forward. This day with my servant, Alan Gefreyson, I sent you my news which are of such bruits, rages, and furies as the like I have not read nor heard of. I sent to my cousin Ellerker and Whartton for the premises concerning Hull. My advice is that you stay the people till the coming of my lord of Norfolk, which, I hear, shall be shortly, and all the gentlemen that is above of the North with him. He brings gracious answers of the Parliament and petitions. Good Mr. Aske, where you write desiring me to stay my quarters; there has yet been no stir in my rooms and lands, but what was caused by other wild countries and dales. I shall do my duty, and play my part therein, though I lie in my bed. I hear my lord of Cumberland is likely to have business for two prisoners he keeps.

Bigod himself wrote to Constable on 18 January:

"Though the commons at first had me in suspicion for my learning and conversation with such a lewd one as they judged were enemies both to Christ's Church and the commonwealth, and I was even in danger of my life at Pountefrett, they have now the greatest confidence in me. Now messengers come from Bishopric, Richmondshire, and the West, for me to go forward with the commons, especially to bring John Halom, whom the mayor of Hull has imprisoned, to their great offence. I have sworn to go with the commons having good reason to doubt the Duke of Norfolk is coming rather to bring them to captivity like those of Lincolnshire than to fulfil our petitions. There is no man they trust so much as Constable whom Bygott would gladly join and follow his advice, if he will be true to them." He begs an answer and sends a copy of their oath.

William Todde, prior of Malton in Ryedale, later gave evidence that on the Tuesday before the uprising, Bigod had dined with him at Malton on his way to York. Bigod had showed him part of the King's pardon, saying it would enrage the Scots, known in the North as "our old ancient enemies", while Todde showed Bigod a copy of the articles given at Doncaster, Bigod asked for a copy, and one was sent after him. On leaving,

Bigod said he had to go to Settrington to meet his brother Ralph.

The rebellion's outcome was that, after its failure, Henry arrested Bigod, Aske and several other rebels, such as Darcy, Thomas Percy and Constable. All were convicted of treason and executed at various locations.

Source http://en.wikipedia.org/wiki/Bigod's_Rebellion

Cornish Rebellion of 1497

Commemorative plaque in Cornish and English for Michael Joseph the Smith (An Gof) and Thomas Flamank mounted on the north side of Blackheath common, south east London, near the south entrance to Greenwich Park

The **Cornish Rebellion of 1497** (Cornish: *Rebellyans Kernow*) was a popular uprising by the people of Cornwall in the far southwest of Britain. Its primary cause was a response of people to the raising of war taxes by King Henry VII on the impoverished Cornish, to raise money for a campaign against Scotland motivated by brief border skirmishes that were inspired by Perkin Warbeck's pretence to the English throne. Tin miners were angered as the scale of the taxes overturned previous rights granted by Edward I of England to the Cornish Stannary Parliament which exempted Cornwall from all taxes of 10ths or 15ths of income.

Background

The primary focus of the Rebellion was protest at Henry VII's tax levy, but the unrest of the Cornish precedes the event by a millennium. Strong Arthurian tradition among the Cornish of the given time period suggests that the people may have viewed the ascendance of the (Welsh) House of Tudor following their success in the Wars of the Roses to the throne as a fulfillment of foretold prophecy. The popular theory appeared true at first with Henry appointing loyal Cornish men to high posts in his court, even naming his first son Arthur and bestowing the title of Duke of Cornwall upon him. However, due to a widening language and cultural gap, popular support for the Crown would not persist.

Rebellion

In reaction to King Henry's tax levy, Michael Joseph (An Gof), a blacksmith from St. Keverne and Thomas Flamank a lawyer of Bodmin, incited many of the people of Cornwall into armed revolt against the King.

An army some 15,000 strong marched into Devon, attracting support in terms of provisions and recruits as they went. Apart from one isolated incident at Taunton, where a tax commissioner was killed, their march was 'without any slaughter, violence or spoil of the country'.

From Taunton, they moved on to Wells, where they were joined by their most eminent recruit, James Touchet, the seventh Baron Audley, a member of the old nobility and an accomplished soldier. Despite this welcome and prestigious acquisition of support, An Gof, the blacksmith, remained in command of the army. Audley joined Thomas Flamank as joint 'political' leader of the expedition.

From Wells to Winchester and Kent

After issuing a declaration of grievances, the army left Wells and marched to Winchester via Bristol and Salisbury, remarkably unopposed as they progressed across the south of England. At this point, having come so far, there seems to have been some questioning of what exactly should be done. The King had shown no sign of willingness to concede the issue and, far from home, there must have come to the leadership the belated cold realisation that only force of arms would resolve the matter one way or the other. Flamank conceived the idea of trying to broaden the rising; to force the monarch into concessions by mobilising wider support for the Cornishmen. He proposed that they should head for Kent, 'the classic soil of protests', the home of the Peasants' Revolt of 1381 and Jack Cade's rebellion, to rally the volatile men of Kent to their banner. It was a subtle and ambitious strategy—but sadly misinformed. Although the Scottish War was as remote a project to the Kentishmen as to the Cornish, they not only declined to offer their support but went so far as to offer resistance under their Earl. Sadly disillusioned, the Cornish army retreated and some of the men quietly returned to their homes. The remainder, let go the pretence of acting against the King's ministers alone - they were prepared to give battle against the King himself.

In Surrey

Moving back west, by Tuesday 13 June 1497 the Cornish army arrived at Guildford. Although shocked by the scale of the revolt and the speed of its approach, Henry VII had not been idle. The army of 8000 men assembled for Scotland under the command of Giles, Lord Daubeney, Henry's chief general and Lord Chamberlain was recalled. Then, by a curious paradox, the Earl of Surrey (the very area under occupation), was sent north to conduct a defensive, holding operation against the Scots until such time as the King had quelled his domestic difficulties. The Royal family (and the Archbishop of Canterbury) moved to the Tower of London for safety whilst in the rest of the City there was panic among the common citizens. It is said there was a general cry of 'Every man to harness! To harness!' and a rush of armed citizenry to the walls and gates. Then, the same day that the Cornish arrived at Guildford, Daubeney and his men took up position upon Hounslow Heath and were cheered by the arrival of food and wine dispatched by the Lord Mayor of London.

The Crown decided to take the offensive and test the strength and resolve of the Cornish forces. Lord Daubeney sent out a force of 500 mounted spearmen and they clashed with the Cornish at 'Gill Down' outside Guildford on Wednesday 14 June 1497.

The Cornish army left Guildford and moved via Banstead and Chussex Plain to Blackheath where they pitched their final camp, looking down from the hill onto the Thames and City of London. Somehow An Gof held his army together, but faced with overwhelming odds, some Cornish deserted and by morning there remained only some 9-10,000 Cornish stalwarts left in arms.

Battle of Deptford Bridge

The Battle of Deptford Bridge (also known as Battle of Blackheath) took place on 17 June 1497 on a site in present-day Deptford south-east London, adjacent to the River Ravensbourne and was the culminating event of the Cornish Rebellion. Henry VII had mustered an army of some 25,000 men and the Cornish lacked the supporting cavalry and artillery arms essential to the professional forces of the time. After carefully spreading rumours that he would attack on the following Monday, Henry moved against the Cornish at dawn on his 'lucky day' - Saturday (17 June 1497). The Royal forces were divided into three 'battles', two under Lords Oxford, Essex and Suffolk, to wheel round the right flank and rear of enemy whilst the third waited in reserve. When the Cornish were duly surrounded, Lord Daubeney and the third 'battle' were ordered into frontal attack.

Cornish force at the bridge

At the bridge at Deptford Strand, the Cornish had placed a body of archers (utilising arrows a full yard long, 'so strong and mighty a bow the Cornishmen were said to draw') to block the passage of the river. Here Daubeney had a tense time, before his spearmen eventually captured the crossing with some losses (a mere 8 men or as many as 300 depending on one's source). The 'Great Chronicle of London' says that these were the only casualties suffered by the Royal forces that day but, in view of the severity of the later fighting, this seems most improbable.

Through ill-advice or inexperience, the Cornish had neglected to provide support for the men at Deptford Strand bridge and the main array stood well back into the heath, near to the top of the hill. This was a mistake since a reserve force charging down from the high ground might have held the bridge bottleneck and made the day a far more equal contest. As it was, Lord Daubeney and his troops poured across in strength and engaged the enemy with great vigour. Daubeney himself was so carried away that he became isolated from his men and was captured. Astoundingly enough, the Cornish simply released him and he soon returned to the fray. It would appear at this late stage, the rebels' hearts were no longer in the battle and they were already contemplating its aftermath and the King's revenge.

Continuation of the battle

The two other Royal divisions attacked the Cornish precisely as planned and, as Bacon succinctly put it: being ill-armed and ill-led, and without horse or artillery, they were with no great difficulty cut in pieces and put to flight. Estimates of the Cornish dead range from 200 to 2000 and a general slaughter of the broken army was well under way when An Gof gave the order for surrender. He fled but only got as far as Greenwich before being captured. The less enterprising Baron Audley and Thomas Flamank were taken on the field of battle.

Aftermath

By 2pm, Henry VII had returned to the City in triumph, knighting deserving parties on the way, to accept the acclamation of the Mayor and attend a service of thanksgiving at St Paul's.

In due course, severe monetary penalties, extracted by Crown agents, pauperised sections of Cornwall for years to come. Prisoners were sold into slavery and estates were seized and handed to more loyal subjects. The remaining rebels that escaped went home ending the rebellion. An Gof and Flamank were both sentenced to the traitor's death of being hanged, drawn and quartered. However they "enjoyed" the king's mercy and were allowed to hang until dead before being decapitated. They were executed at Tyburn on 27 June 1497. An Gof is recorded to have said before his execution that he should have *"a name perpetual and a fame permanent and immortal"*. Thomas Flamank was quoted as saying *"Speak the truth and only then can you be free of your chains"*.

Audley, as a peer of the realm, was beheaded on the 28th June at Tower Hill. Their heads were then displayed on pike-staffs ("gibbeted") on London Bridge.

Quincentennial

Keskerdh Kernow *(Cornish: Cornwall marches on!)* was a commemorative march which retraced the original route of the Cornish from St. Keverne to Blackheath, London, to celebrate the Quincentennial—500th anniversary—of the Cornish Rebellion.

A statue depicting the Cornish leaders, "Michael An Gof" and Thomas Flamank was unveiled at An Gof's village of St. Keverne and a commemorative plaque was also unveiled on Blackheath common.

Cultural references

The rebellion is referred to several times in *Wolf Hall*, the 2009 Man Booker Prize winner written by Hilary Mantel. The protagonist of the book, Thomas Cromwell, is a young boy in London during the panic caused by the approach of the rebels; he also remembers the events later in the book.

Source http://en.wikipedia.org/wiki/Cornish_Rebellion_of_1497

Desmond Rebellions

The **Desmond Rebellions** occurred in 1569-1573 and 1579-1583 in the Irish province of Munster.

They were rebellions by the Earl of Desmond – head of the FitzGerald dynasty in Munster – and his followers, the Geraldines and their allies against the threat of the extension of their Anglicised South Welsh Tewdwr cousin's, Elizabethan English government over the province. The rebellions were motivated primarily by the desire to maintain the independence of feudal lords from their monarch, but also had an element of religious antagonism between Catholic Geraldines and the Protestant English state. The result was the destruction of the Desmond dynasty and the subsequent plantation or colonisation of Munster with English settlers. 'Desmond' is the Anglicisation given to the Irish *Deasmumhain*, which translates to 'South Munster'.

Causes

The south of Ireland (the provinces of Munster and southern Leinster) was dominated, as it had been for over two centuries, by the Old English Butlers of Ormonde and the FitzGeralds of Desmond, who maintained feudal principalities. Both houses raised their own armed forces and imposed their own law, a mixture of Irish and English customs independent of the English government of Ireland. Beginning in the 1530s, successive English administrations in Ireland tried to expand English control over the entire island (See Tudor conquest of Ireland). By the 1560s, their attention had turned to the south of Ireland and Henry Sidney, as Lord Deputy of Ireland, was charged with establishing the authority of the English government over the independent lordships there. His solution was the formation of "lord presidencies"—provincial military governors who would replace the local lords as military powers and keepers of the peace.

The local dynasties saw the presidencies as intrusions into their sphere of influence, and into their traditional violent competition with each other. This had seen the Butlers and FitzGeralds fight a pitched battle against each other at Affane in County Waterford in 1565. This was a blatant defiance of the Elizabethan state's law. Elizabeth I summoned the heads of both houses to London to explain their actions. However, the treatment of the dynasties was not even handed. Thomas Butler, 3rd Earl of Ormonde — who was the Queen's cousin — was pardoned, while both Gerald FitzGerald, 14th Earl of Desmond (in 1567) and his brother, John of Desmond, widely regarded as the real military leader of the FitzGeralds, (in 1568) were arrested and detained in the Tower of London on Ormonde's urging.

This decapitated the natural leadership of the Munster Geraldines and left the Desmond Earldom in the hands of a soldier, James FitzMaurice FitzGerald, the "captain general" of the Desmond military. Fitzmaurice had little stake in a new de-militarised order in Munster, which envisaged the abolition of the Irish lords' private armies. A factor that drew wider support for Fitzmaurice was the prospect of land confiscations, which had been mooted by Sidney and Peter Carew, an English claimant to lands granted to an ancestor just after the Norman conquest of Ireland that were lost soon afterwards.

This ensured Fitzmaurice the support of important clans, notably MacCarthy Mor, O'Sullivan Beare and O'Keefe and two prominent Butlers –brothers of the Earl. Fitzmaurice himself had lost the land he had held at Kerricurrihy in County Cork, which had been leased instead to English colonists. He was also a devout Catholic, influenced by the counter-reformation, which made him see the Protestant Elizabethan governors as his enemies. To discourage Sidney from going ahead with the Lord Presidency for Munster and to re-establish Desmond primacy over the Butlers, he planned a rebellion against the English presence in the south and against the Earl of Ormonde. Fitzmaurice however had wider aims than simply the recovery of FitzGerald supremacy within the context of the English Kingdom of Ireland. Before the rebellion, he secretly sent Maurice MacGibbon, Catholic Archbishop of Cashel, to seek military aid from Philip II of Spain.

First Desmond Rebellion

First Desmond Rebellion
Part of the Desmond Rebellions

Date June 1569 – 23 February 1573
Location Province of Munster, Ireland
Result English victory

Second Desmond Rebellion

Belligerents

FitzGeralds of Desmond	Kingdom of England
allied Irish clans	Kingdom of Ireland
	allied Irish clans

Commanders and leaders

-James FitzMaurice FitzGerald	-Henry Sidney
	-Thomas Butler
	-Humphrey Gilbert
	-John Perrot (1571–1573)

Strength
? ?

Casualties and losses
? ?

Fitzmaurice launched his rebellion by attacking the English colony at Kerrycurihy south of Cork city in June 1569 before attacking Cork itself and those native lords who refused to join the rebellion. Fitzmaurice's force of up to 4,500 men went on to besiege Kilkenny, seat of the Earls of Ormonde in July. In response, Sidney mobilised 600 English troops, who marched south from Dublin and another 400 troops landed by sea in Cork. Thomas Butler, Earl of Ormonde returned from London, where he had been at court, brought the rebel Butlers out of the rebellion and mobilised Gaelic Irish clans antagonistic to the Geraldines. Together, Ormonde, Sidney and Humphrey Gilbert, appointed as governor of Munster, began devastating the lands of Fitzmaurice's allies. Fitzmaurice's forces broke up, as individual lords had to retire to defend their own territories. Gilbert in particular was notorious for the terror tactics he employed, killing civilians at random and setting up corridors of severed heads at the entrance to his camps.

Sidney forced Fitzmaurice into the mountains of Kerry, from where he launched hit and run attacks on the English and their allies. By 1570, most of Fitzmaurice's allies had submitted to Sidney. The most important, Donal MacCarthy Mor, surrendered in November 1569. Nevertheless, the guerrilla campaign dragged on for three more years. In February 1571, John Perrot was made Lord President of Munster, pursuing Fitzmaurice with 700 troops for over a year without success. Fitzmaurice had some victories, capturing an English ship near Kinsale and burning the town of Kilmallock in 1571, for example, but by early 1573, his force was reduced to less than 100 men. Fitzmaurice finally submitted on February 23, 1573, having negotiated a pardon for his life. However in 1574, he again became landless and in 1575 he sailed to France to seek help from the Catholic powers to start another rebellion.

Gerald FitzGerald, Earl of Desmond, and his brother John were released from prison to stabilise the situation and to reconstruct their shattered territory. Under a new settlement imposed after the rebellion, known as "composition", the Desmond's military forces were limited by law to just 20 horsemen; their tenants were made to pay rent to them rather supply military service or to quarter their soldiers. Perhaps the biggest winner of the first Desmond Rebellion was the Earl of Ormonde, who established himself as loyal to the English Crown and as the most powerful lord in the south of Ireland.

Although all of the local chiefs had submitted by the end of the rebellion, the methods used to suppress it provoked lingering resentment, especially among the Irish mercenaries; *gall oglaigh* or "gallowglass" as the English termed them, who had rallied to Fitzmaurice. William Drury, the new Lord President of Munster from 1576, executed around 700 of them in the years after the rebellion. Furthermore, in the aftermath of the rebellion, Gaelic customs such as Brehon Laws, Irish dress, bardic poetry and the maintaining of private armies were again outlawed – things that were highly provocative to traditional Irish society. Fitzmaurice, by contrast, had deliberately emphasised the Gaelic character of the rebellion, wearing the Irish dress, speaking only Irish and referring to himself as the captain (*taoiseach*) of the Geraldines. Finally, Irish landowners continued to be threatened by the arrival of English colonists. All of these factors meant that, when Fitzmaurice returned from continental Europe to start a new rebellion, there were plenty of discontented people in Munster waiting to join him.

In late 1569 a similar Catholic rebellion, the "Northern Rebellion," broke out in England, but was quickly crushed. This and the Desmond Rebellion caused the Pope to issue "Regnans in Excelsis", excommunicating Elizabeth and depriving her of the allegiance of her Catholic subjects, in early 1570. Elizabeth's regime had previously accepted discreet Roman Catholic worship in private; afterwards it suppressed organised Catholicism more severely.

Second Desmond Rebellion

The second Desmond rebellion was sparked when James Fitzmaurice FitzGerald launched an invasion of Munster in 1579. During his exile in Europe, he had reinvented himself as a soldier of the counter-reformation, arguing that since the Pope's excommunication of Elizabeth I in 1570 Irish Catholics no longer owed loyalty to a heretic monarch. The Pope granted Fitzmaurice an "indulgence" and supplied him with troops and money. Fitzmaurice landed at Smerwick, near Dingle (modern County Kerry) on July 18, 1579 with a small force of Spanish and Italian troops. He was joined in rebellion on August 1 by John of Desmond, a brother of the Earl, who had a large following among his kinsmen and the disaffected swordsmen of Munster. Other Gaelic clans and Old English families also joined in the rebellion. After Fitzmaurice was killed in a skirmish with the Clanwilliam Burkes on 18 August, John FitzGerald assumed leadership of the rebellion.

Carrigafoyle Castle

Gerald, the Earl of Desmond, initially resisted the call of the rebels and tried to remain neutral but gave in once the authorities had proclaimed him a traitor. The Earl joined the rebellion by sacking the towns of Youghal (on November 13) and Kinsale, and devastated the country of the English and their allies. However, by the summer of 1580, English troops under William Pelham and locally raised Irish forces under the Earl of Ormonde succeeded in bringing the rebellion under control, re-taking the south coast, destroying the lands of the Desmonds and their allies in the process, and killing their tenants. By capturing Carrigafoyle at Easter 1580, the principal Desmond castle at the mouth of Shannon river, they cut off the Geraldine forces from the rest of the country and prevented a landing of foreign troops into the main Munster ports. It looked as if the rebellion was fizzling out.

However, in July 1580, the rebellion spread to Leinster, under the leadership of Gaelic Irish chieftain Fiach MacHugh O'Byrne and the Pale lord Viscount Baltinglass, both motivated by Catholicism and hostility to the English administration. A large English force under the Lord Deputy of Ireland Earl Grey de Wilton was sent to subdue them, only to be ambushed and massacred at the battle of Glenmalure on 25 August, losing over 800 dead. However, the Leinster rebels were unable to capitalise on their victory or to effectively coordinate their strategy with the Munster insurgents.

On 10 September 1580, 600 papal troops landed at Smerwick in Kerry to support the rebellion, but were besieged in a fort at Dún an Óir. They surrendered after two days of bombardment and were then massacred. By relentless scorched-earth tactics, the English broke the momentum of the rebellion by mid 1581. By May 1581, most of the minor rebels and FitzGerald allies in Munster and Leinster had accepted Elizabeth I's offer of a general pardon. John of Desmond, in many ways the main leader of the rebellion, was killed north of Cork in early 1582.

For the Geraldine Earl however there could be no second pardon, and he was pursued by crown forces until the end. From 1581 to 1583, the war dragged on, with his supporters evading capture in the mountains of Kerry. The rebellion was finally ended on 2 November 1583 when the earl was hunted down and killed near Tralee in Kerry by the local clan O'Moriarty. The clan chief, Maurice, received 1000 pounds of silver from the English government for Desmond's head, which was sent to Queen Elizabeth. His body was triumphantly displayed on the walls of Cork.

Aftermath

After three years of scorched earth warfare, famine hit Munster. In April 1582, the provost marshal of Munster, Sir Warham St Leger, estimated that 30,000 people had died of famine in the previous six months. Plague broke out in Cork city, where the country people fled to avoid the fighting. People continued to die of famine and plague long after the war had ended, and it is estimated that by 1589 one third of the province's population had died. Grey was recalled by Elizabeth I for his excessive brutality. Two famous accounts tell us of the devastation of Munster after the Desmond rebellion. The first is from the Gaelic Annals of the Four Masters:

" *... the whole tract of country from Waterford to Lothra, and from Cnamhchoill to the county of Kilkenny, was suffered to remain one surface of weeds and waste... At this period it was commonly said, that the lowing of a cow, or the whistle of the ploughboy, could scarcely be heard from Dun-Caoin to Cashel in Munster.* "

The second is from the **View of the Present State of Ireland**, written by English poet Edmund Spenser, who fought in the campaign:

" *In those late wars in Munster; for notwithstanding that the same was a most rich and plentiful country, full of corn and cattle, that you would have thought they could have been able to stand long, yet ere one year and a half they were brought to such wretchedness, as that any stony heart would have rued the same. Out of every corner of the wood and glens they came creeping forth upon their hands, for their legs could not bear them; they looked Anatomies [of] death, they spoke like ghosts, crying out of their graves; they did eat of the carrions, happy where they could find them, yea, and one another soon after, in so much as the very carcasses they spared not to scrape out of their graves; and if they found a plot of water-cresses or shamrocks, there they flocked as to a feast for the time, yet not able long to continue therewithal; that in a short space there were none almost left, and a most populous and plentiful country suddenly left void of man or beast.* "

The wars of the 1570s and 1580s marked a watershed in Ireland. Although English control over the country was still far from total, the southern Geraldine axis of power had been annihilated, and Munster was "planted" with English colonists following the parliamentary arrangements of 1585. Following a survey begun in 1584 by Sir Valentine Browne, Surveyor General of Ireland, the thousands of English soldiers and administrators who had been imported to deal with the rebellion were allocated land in the Munster Plantation of Desmond's confiscated estates. The Elizabethan conquest of Ireland was completed after the subsequent Nine Years War in Ulster and the extension of plantation policy to other parts of the country.

Source http://en.wikipedia.org/wiki/Desmond_Rebellions

Exeter Conspiracy

The **Exeter Conspiracy**, 1538, was a supposed attempt to depose the reigning Henry VIII and replace him with a Yorkist, Henry Courtenay, 1st Marquess of Exeter, KG who was 1st cousin to the King. An Act of Attainder was brought against the Marquess of Exeter and he was found guilty of treason by his peers in Westminster Hall, along with other supposed conspirators. Some sources suggest the 'conspiracy' was largely exaggerated by Thomas Cromwell, at this point Chancellor of the Exchequer, and Richard Rich, 1st Baron Rich. Victorian historian J. A. Froude, however, writes that the Courtenays were 'petty sovereigns in Devonshire and Cornwall', which may go some way to explaining the true nature of the conspiracy. Yet there is no evidence to suggest that Courtenay ever had the means to or intended to muster any kind of rebellion against the King, the charges brought against Lord Exeter were based on the correspondence he had with Cardinal Pole and the testimony of Sir Geoffrey Pole, whose brother Henry Pole, 1st Baron Montagu was also arrested and beheaded alongside Courtenay and another supposed plotter Sir Nicholas Carew KG, the Master of the Horse to Henry VIII on 9 December 1538 on Tower Hill.

Theatrical Depictions

The events of the 'Exeter Conspiracy' were dramatised for the stage in a play called *Our Father/Pater Noster* (2009). It took place in May 2009 at St Nicholas' Priory in Exeter.
Source http://en.wikipedia.org/wiki/Exeter_Conspiracy

Jack of the North

Jack of The North identifies an otherwise untitled, short dialogue responding to and supporting anti-enclosure actions in Cambridgeshire in 1549, the year before Kett's Rebellion. The text is printed in Charles Henry Cooper's *Annals of Cambridge*, which names the source as "Dr. Lamb's Cambridge Documents". The dialogue participants are Jack of the North beyond the style, Robbyn Clowte, Tom of Trompington, Buntynge on the Hyll, Peter Potter, Pyrse Plowman, Symon Slater, Harry Clowte, Whyp Wylliam, and Hodge Hasteler. The two Clowtes and Pyrse Plowman were established poetic personnae from John Skelton and William Langland; both would later appear in the poetry of Edmund Spenser.

Navigation menu

Personal tools
Create account

Log in

Namespaces
Article
Talk

Variants

Actions

Search

Navigation
Main page
Contents
Featured content
Current events
Random article
Donate to Wikipedia

Interaction
Help
About Wikipedia
Community portal
Recent changes
Contact Wikipedia

Toolbox
What links here
Related changes
Upload file
Special pages
Permanent link
Page information
Cite this page

Print/export
Create a book
Download as PDF
Printable version

Languages
Edit links
Source http://en.wikipedia.org/wiki/Jack_of_the_North

Kett's Rebellion

Kett's Rebellion was a revolt in Norfolk, England during the reign of Edward VI, largely in response to the enclosure of land. It began at Wymondham on 8 July 1549 with a group of rebels destroying fences that had been put up by wealthy landowners. One of their targets was yeoman farmer Robert Kett who, instead of resisting the rebels, agreed to their demands and offered to lead them. Kett and his forces, joined by recruits from Norwich and the surrounding countryside and numbering some 16,000, set up camp on Mousehold Heath to the north-east of the city on 12 July. The rebels stormed Norwich on 21 July and on 1 August defeated a force led by the Marquess of Northampton that had been sent by the government to suppress the uprising. Kett's rebellion ended on 27 August when the rebels were defeated by an army under the leadership of the Earl of Warwick at the Battle of Dussindale. Kett was captured, held in the Tower of London, tried for treason, and hanged from Norwich Castle on 7 December 1549.

Background to the rebellion

The 1540s saw a crisis in agriculture in England. With the majority of the population depending on the land, this led to outbreaks of unrest across the country. Kett's rebellion in Norfolk was the most serious of these. The main grievance of the rioters was enclosure, the fencing-off of common land by landlords for their own use. Enclosure left peasants with nowhere to graze their animals. Some landowners were forcing tenants off their farms so that they could engross their holdings and convert arable land into pasture for sheep, which had become more profitable as demand for wool increased. Inflation,

An 18th century depiction of Robert Kett and his followers under the Oak of Reformation on Mousehold Heath

Kett's Rebellion is remembered on Wymondham's town sign

Kett's Oak, beside the B1172, near Hethersett, Norfolk

unemployment, rising rents and declining wages added to the hardships faced by the common people. As one historian put it, they "could scarcely doubt that the state had been taken over by a breed of men whose policy was to rob the poor for the benefit of the rich".

Uprising at Wymondham

Kett's rebellion, or "the commotion time" as it was also called in Norfolk, began in July 1549 in the small market town of Wymondham, nearly ten miles south-west of Norwich. The previous month there had been a minor disturbance at the nearby town of Attleborough where fences, built by the lord of the manor to enclose common lands, were torn down. The rioters thought they were acting legally, since the king had issued a proclamation against illegal enclosures. Wymondham held its annual feast on the weekend of 6 July 1549 and a play in honour of St Thomas Becket, the co-patron of Wymondham Abbey, was performed. This celebration was illegal, as Henry VIII had decreed in 1538 that the name of Thomas Becket should be removed from the church calendar. On the Monday, when the feast was over, a group of people set off to the villages of Morley St. Botolph and Hethersett to tear down hedges and fences. One of their first targets was Sir John Flowerdew, a lawyer and landowner at Hethersett who was unpopular for his role as overseer of the demolition of Wymondham Abbey (part of which was the parish church) during the dissolution of the monasteries and for enclosing land. Flowerdew bribed the rioters to leave his enclosures alone and instead attack those of Robert Kett at Wymondham.

Kett was about 57 years old and was one of the wealthier farmers in Wymondham. The Ketts (also spelt Ket, Cat, Chat, or Knight) had been farming in Norfolk since the twelfth century. Kett was the son of Tom and Margery Kett and had several brothers, and clergyman Francis Kett was his nephew. Two or possibly three of Kett's brothers were dead by 1549, but his eldest brother William joined him in the rebellion. Kett's wife, Alice, and several sons are not recorded as having been involved in the rebellion. Kett had been prominent among the parishioners in saving their parish church when Wymondham Abbey was demolished and this had led to conflict with Flowerdew. Having listened to the rioters' grievances, Kett decided to join their cause and helped them tear down his own fences before taking them back to Hethersett where they destroyed Flowerdew's enclosures. Sir John Hayward, *Life of King Edward VI*

The following day, Tuesday 9 July, the protesters set off for Norwich. By now Kett was their leader and they were being joined by people from nearby towns and villages. A meeting point for the rebels was an oak tree on the road from Hethersett to Norwich. Known as Kett's Oak, it has been preserved by Norfolk County Council, and a new plaque was unveiled in 2006. The oak became a symbol of the rebellion when an oak tree on Mousehold Heath was made the centre of the rebel camp, but this "Oak of Reformation" no longer stands.

Mousehold camp

Kett and his followers camped for the night of 9 July at Bowthorpe, just west of Norwich. Here they were approached by the sheriff of Norfolk and Suffolk, Sir Edmund Wyndham, who ordered them to disperse. The response was negative, and the sheriff retreated back to Norwich. Next the rebels were visited by the mayor of Norwich, Thomas Codd, who met a similar response. The following night the rebels camped at nearby Eaton Wood and then, having been refused permission to march through Norwich to reach Mousehold Heath north-east of the city, crossed the River Wensum at Hellesdon and spent the night at Drayton. On Friday 12 July the rebels reached Mousehold, where they had a vantage point overlooking Norwich, and set up the camp that was their base for the next six and a half weeks. The camp was the largest of several rebel camps that had appeared in East Anglia that summer. The rebels were known at the time as the "camp men" and the rebellion as the "camping tyme" or "commotion tyme".

An early 19th century painting of Mousehold Heath by local artist John Crome

Kett set up his headquarters in St Michael's Chapel, the ruins of which have since been known as Kett's Castle. Mount Surrey, a house built by the Earl of Surrey on the site of the despoiled St Leonard's Priory, had lain empty since the Earl's execution in 1547 and was used to hold Kett's prisoners. Kett's council, which consisted of representatives from the Hundreds of Norfolk and one representative from Suffolk met under the Oak of Reformation to administer the camp, issuing warrants to obtain provisions and arms and arrest members of the gentry. According to one source the Oak of Reformation was cut down by Norwich City Council in the 1960s to make way for a car park, although Reg Groves wrote in the 1940s that had already been destroyed. The camp was joined by workers and artisans from Norwich, and by people from the surrounding towns and villages, until it was larger than Norwich, at that time the second-largest city in England with a population of about 12,000. The city authorities, having sent messengers to London, remained in negotiation with the rebels and Mayor Thomas Codd, former Mayor Thomas Aldrich and preacher Robert Watson accepted the rebels' invitation to take part in their council.

Once the camp was established at Mousehold the rebels drew up a list of 29 grievances, signed by Kett, Codd, Aldrich and the representatives of the Hundreds, and sent it to Protector Somerset. The grievances have been described by one historian as a shopping-list of demands but which nevertheless have a strong logic underlying them, articulating "a desire to limit the power of the gentry, exclude them from the world of the village, constrain rapid economic change, prevent the overexploitation of communal resources, and remodel the values of the clergy". Although the rebels were all the while tearing down hedges and filling in ditches, only one of the 29 articles mentioned enclosure: "We pray your grace that where it is enacted for inclosyng that it be not hurtfull to suche as have enclosed saffren grounds for they be grely chargeablye to them, and that from hensforth noman shall enclose any more". The exemption for saffron grounds has puzzled historians; one has suggested that it may have been a scribal error for "sovereign grounds", grounds that were the exclusive freehold property of their owners, while others have commented on the importance of saffron to local industry. The rebels also "pray[ed] that all bonde men may be made ffre for god made all ffre with his precious blode sheddyng." The rebels may have been articulating a grievance against the 1547 *Act for the Punishment of Vagabonds*, which made it legal to enslave a discharged servant who did not find a new master within three days, though they may also have been calling for the manumission of the thousands of Englishmen and women who were serfs. (In 1549, an *Act Touching on the Punishment of Vagabonds and Other Idle Persons* avoided the word "slave" but retained many of the harshest provisions of the 1547 *Act*.)

The truce between the city and the camp was ended on 21 July by a messenger from the King's Council, York Herald Bartholomew Butler, who arrived at Norwich from London, went with city officials to Mousehold, proclaimed the gathering a rebellion, and offered pardon. Kett rejected the offer, saying he had no need of a pardon because he had committed no treason. York Herald lacked the forces to arrest the rebels and retreated into Norwich with the Mayor. Kett and his followers were now officially rebels; the authorities therefore shut the city gates and set about preparing the city defences.

Fall of Norwich

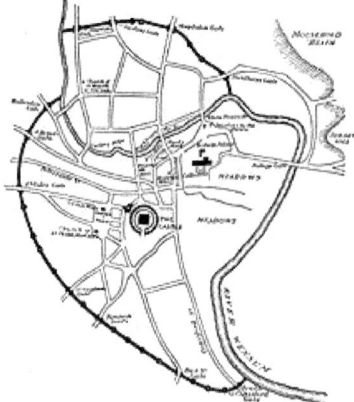

Norwich at the time of Kett's Rebellion

Kett was now left with a decision. He would not, probably could not, disperse the camp, but without access to the markets of Norwich, his people would starve. It was therefore decided to attack Norwich.

In the late evening of 21 July 1549, rebel artillery positioned on and beneath Mount Surrey, the heights opposite the Bishopsgate bridge, at the top of which now stands a memorial to the rebellion, opened fire. The bombardment and the response from the city's artillery entrenched next to the bridge and around the Cow Tower lasted through the night.

At first light on 22 July, Kett withdrew his artillery. The city defenders had repositioned six artillery pieces in the meadow behind the hospital (now the cricket ground of Norwich school) and were laying down such an accurate fire that the rebels feared the loss of all their guns. Under a flag of truce the rebels demanded access to the city, which the city authorities refused.

Kett's artillery, now on the slopes of Mousehold Heath, opened fire on the city. The guns in the hospital meadow could not reach far enough uphill to return the fire. At this point an assault began, ordered by Kett or perhaps by other rebel leaders. Thousands of rebels charged down from Mousehold and began swimming the Wensum between the Cow Tower and Bishops Gate. The city defenders fired volleys of arrows into the rebels as they crossed, but could not stop the attack. A running battle ensued. In the market square the York Herald tried to address the rebels, but as threats were made against him he fled in fear of his life. England's second city was in the hands of a rebel army.

Attacks on the rebels

The King sent the Marquess of Northampton with 1,500 men, including Italian mercenaries, to quell the rebellion. As he drew near to the city he sent forward his herald to demand the surrender of the city. The Deputy Mayor, Augustine Steward, responded. It was conveyed that the rebels had retreated back to the safety of the high ground overlooking the city. Kett had already seen how difficult it was to defend miles of walls and gates and had instead chosen to withdraw. It was much more prudent to allow Northampton's tiny army to defend the city while he again laid siege to it.

On the night of 31 July the Royal army made its defensive preparations and started patrolling the city's narrow streets. Around midnight alarms rang out, waking Northampton. It appeared hundreds of rebels were using the cover of darkness and their knowledge of the maze of small streets and alleys around Tombland to launch hit-and-run attacks on Royal troops. Lord Sheffield suggested constructing ramparts along the eastern side of the city, which was open to attack, and warned that the rebels were crossing the river around Bishopsgate with ease.

By 8 am the following morning, 1 August, the ramparts were strengthened between the Cow Tower and Bishopsgate, so Sheffield retired to The Maid's Head inn for breakfast. A little after this, Northampton received information that the rebels wished to discuss surrender and were gathering around the Pockthorpe gate. Sheffield went with the Herald to discuss this apparent good turn of events with the rebels. On arrival, Sheffield found no rebels at all. It appears to have been either a false rumour or a diversion, as at that point thousands of rebels again began crossing the River Wensum around Bishopsgate.

Northampton's main force was in the market place. As the attack developed, he fed men through the streets into a growing and vicious street battle across the whole eastern area of the city. Seeing things going the rebels' way, Sheffield took command of a body of cavalry and charged the rebels across the cathedral precinct, past St Martin at Place Church and into Bishopsgate Street. Outside the Great Hospital in Bishopsgate Street, Sheffield fell from his horse into a ditch. Expecting then to be captured and ransomed, as was the custom, he removed his helmet, only to be killed by a blow from a rebel, reputedly a butcher named Fulke.

With the loss of a senior commander and his army being broken up in street fighting, Northampton ordered a retreat. The retreat did not stop until the remnants of the Royal Army reached Cambridge. Somerset himself had judged the Norfolk "commotion" a minor affair, to be dealt with a small contingent of troops. Now, he blamed Northampton for tactical errors and poor leadership, while remaining undecided on how to proceed further.

The Earl of Warwick was then sent with a stronger army of around 14,000 men including mercenaries from Wales, Germany and Spain. Warwick had previously fought in France, was a former member of the House of Commons and subsequently the Privy Council, making him a strong leader. Despite the increased threat, the rebels were loyal to Kett throughout and continued to fight Warwick's men.

Northampton served as Warwick's second-in-command in the second attempt to deal with the rebel host, this time with a much larger force. Northampton's renewed appointment "gave Warwick the benefit of the former's knowledge of conditions at Nor-

The Earl of Warwick led the force that defeated the rebels

wich and reaffirmed his judgment that the earlier debacle had not been entirely the result of Northampton's mismanagement."

Warwick managed to enter the city on 24 August by attacking the St Stephen's and Brazen gates. The rebels retreated through the city, setting fire to houses as they went in an attempt to slow the Royal army's advance. About 3 pm Warwick's baggage train entered the city. It managed to get lost and rather than halting in the market place it continued through Tombland and straight down Bishopsgate Street towards the rebel army. A group of rebels saw the train from Mousehold and ran down into the city to capture it. Captain Drury led his men in an attempt to recapture the train, which included all the artillery. He managed to salvage some of the guns in yet another fierce fight around Bishopsgate.

At 10 pm that same night shouts of "fire" started. The rebels had entered the city and were burning it. Warwick was in the same trap as Northampton had been, surrounded inside a city in danger of being burnt to the ground.

At first light on 25 August the rebels changed tactics. Their artillery broke down the walls around the northern area of the city near the Magdalen and Pockthorpe gates. With the north of the city again in rebel hands, Warwick launched an attack. Bitter street fighting eventually cleared the city once again. The rebels bombarded the city throughout the day and night.

On 26 August, 1,500 foreign mercenaries arrived in the city. These were German "landsknechts", a mix of handgunners and pikemen. With these reinforcements and the townsfolk, Warwick now had an army so formidable it could no longer hide within the city. Kett and his people were aware of this, and that night they left their camp at Mousehold for lower ground in preparation for battle.

During the morning of 27 August, the armies faced each other outside the city. The final battle took place at *Dussindale*, and was a disaster for the rebels. In the open, against well-armed and trained troops, thousands were killed and the rest ran for their lives.

The location of Dussindale has never been established. The most popular theory is that the dale began in the vicinity of the Plumstead Road East allotments that swept into Valley Drive and into the present remnant of Mousehold, into the Long Valley and out into what is now Gertrude Road and the allotments. In Victorian times this area was known as 'Ketts Meadow'. The name Dussindale has been given to a recent housing development in nearby Thorpe St Andrew.

Aftermath

About 3,000 rebels are thought to have been killed at Dussindale, with Warwick's army losing some 250 men. The morning after the battle, 28 August, rebels were hanged at the Oak of Reformation and outside the Magdalen Gate. Estimates of the number vary from 30 to 300. Warwick had already executed 49 rebels when he had entered Norwich a few days before. There is only one attested incident in which the rebels had killed in cold blood: one of Northampton's Italian mercenaries had been hanged following his capture.

Kett was captured at the village of Swannington the night after the battle and taken, together with his brother William, to the Tower of London to await trial for treason. Found guilty, the brothers were returned to Norwich at the beginning of December. Kett was hanged from the walls of Norwich Castle on 7 December 1549; on the same day William was hanged from the west tower of Wymondham Abbey.

Legacy

Plaque on the wall of Norwich Castle
In 1550 the Norwich authorities decreed that in future 27 August should be a holiday to commemorate "the deliverance of the city" from Kett's Rebellion, and paid for lectures in the cathedral and parish churches on the sins of rebellion. This tradition continued for over a century.

The only known surviving eye-witness account of the rebellion, a manuscript by Nicholas Sotherton, son of a Norwich mayor, is hostile towards the rebels. So too is Alexander Neville's 1575 Latin history of the rebellion, *De furoribus Norfolciensium*. Neville was secretary to Matthew Parker, who had preached to Kett's followers under the Oak of Reformation on Mousehold, unsuccessfully appealing to them to disperse. In 1615 Neville's work was translated into English by Norfolk clergyman Richard Woods under the title *Norfolke Furies* and was reprinted throughout the following century. Kett's name was thus kept alive as a "reviled symbol of rustic violence". It was only in the 19th century that more sympathetic portrayals of the rebellion appeared in print and started the process that saw Kett transformed from traitor to folk hero. An anonymous work of 1843 was critical of Neville's account of the rebellion, and in 1859 clergyman Frederic Russell, who had unearthed new material in archives for his account of the rebellion, concluded that "though Kett is commonly considered a rebel, yet the cause he advocated is so just, that one cannot but feel he deserved a better name and a better fate".

In 1948 Alderman Fred Henderson, a former mayor of Norwich who had been imprisoned in the Castle for his part in the food riots of 1885, proposed a memorial to Kett. Originally hoping for a statue, he settled for a plaque on

Robert Kett's death is commemorated in 2011

the walls of Norwich Castle engraved with his words and unveiled in 1949, 400 years after the rebellion. In the 21st century the death of Kett is still remembered by the people of Norwich. On 7 December 2011, the anniversary of his death, a memorial march by members of Norwich *Occupy* and Norwich Green Party took place and a wreath was laid by the gates of Norwich Castle.

The Oak of Reformation on Kett House, an office block in Station Road, Cambridge

After the rebellion the lands of Kett and his brother William were forfeited, although some of them were later restored to one of his sons. In the longer term the Kett family do not seem to have suffered from their association with the rebellion, but to have prospered in various parts of Norfolk. George Kett, a descendant of Kett's younger brother Thomas, moved to Cambridge and co-founded the architectural masonry company of Rattee & Kett. George Kett's son, also George, was mayor of Cambridge on three occasions and compiled a genealogy of the Kett family.

The rebellion is remembered in the names of schools, streets, pubs and a walking route in the Norwich and Wymondham area, including the Robert Kett Junior School in Wymondham, Dussindale Primary School in Norwich, the Robert Kett pub in Wymondham and Kett's Tavern in Norwich, and in a folk band, Lewis Garland and Kett's Rebellion, and a beer, Kett's Rebellion, by Woodforde's Brewery in Norwich.

Kett's rebellion has featured in novels, including Frederick H. Moore's *Mistress Haselwode: A tale of the Reformation Oak* (1876)), F.C. Tansley's *For Kett and Countryside* (1910), Jack Lindsay's *The Great Oak* (1949), Sylvia Haymon's children's story *The Loyal Traitor* (1965), and Margaret Callow's *A Rebellious Oak* (2012); plays, including George Colman Green's *Kett the tanner* (1909); and poetry, including Keith Chandler's collection *Kett's Rebellion and Other Poems* (1982). In 1988 British composer Malcolm Arnold produced the *Robert Kett Overture (Opus 141)*, inspired by the rebellion.

Notes and references

Source http://en.wikipedia.org/wiki/Kett's_Rebellion

List of Tudor Rebellions

The **List of Tudor Rebellions** refers to various movements which attempted to resist the authority of the Tudor Monarchs, who ruled over England and parts of Ireland between 1485 and 1603. Some of these were the product of religious grievances (for example Wyatt's Rebellion), some were regional or ethnic in nature (e.g. the Cornish Rebellion of 1497), though most combined an element of both (such as the Prayer Book Rebellion in the West Country of England and the Desmond Rebellions in southern Ireland).

The last and greatest of the major Tudor rebellions was Tyrone's Rebellion, more commonly referred to as the Nine Years' War.

Chronology of Tudor Rebellions:1485-1603

1486 - Stafford and Lovell Rebellion
1486-7 - Simnel Rebellion
1489 - Yorkshire Rebellion
1497 - Cornish Rebellion of 1497
1497 - Warbeck Rebellion
1525 - Amicable Grant
1534-7 - Silken Thomas Rebellion (Kildare Rebellion)
1536-7 - Pilgrimage of Grace
1549 - Prayer Book Rebellion (Western)
1549 - Kett's Rebellion
1553 - Northumberland Rebellion
1554 - Wyatt's rebellion
1558-67 - Shane O'Neill Rebellion
1569 - Rising of the North (Northern Earls)
1569-73 - First Desmond Rebellion(Munster)
1579-83 - Second Desmond Rebellion (Geraldine)
1594-1603 - Tyrone's Rebellion(Nine Years' War)
1596 - Oxfordshire Rebellion
1601 - Essex Rebellion

Navigation menu

Personal tools
Create account
Log in

Namespaces
Article
Talk

Variants

Actions

Search

Navigation
Main page
Contents
Featured content
Current events
Random article
Donate to Wikipedia

Interaction
Help
About Wikipedia
Community portal
Recent changes
Contact Wikipedia

Toolbox
What links here
Related changes
Upload file
Special pages
Permanent link
Page information
Cite this page

Print/export
Create a book
Download as PDF
Printable version

Languages
Edit links
Source http://en.wikipedia.org/wiki/List_of_Tudor_Rebellions

Oxfordshire Rising of 1596

The **Oxfordshire Rising** took place in November 1596 under the rule of Queen Elizabeth I of England during times of bad harvest and unprecedented poverty. A small group of impoverished men developed a plan to seize weapons and armour and march on London, hoping to attract "200 or 300... from various towns of that shire". They met on Enslow Hill on November 21st, but without any of the assumed support were quickly arrested, and tortured due to suspicions of a wider conspiracy. A year later two of the men were hung, drawn and quartered for their treason.

Background

The years 1596-8 were the worst for many years for the English population, as bad harvests coincided with outbreaks of disease, as well as a fall in wages which forced many people into starvation. Given the state of the poorest classes, those with property felt threatened by revolt, a fact not helped by the boom in publishing of sensationalist literature detailing the many 'crimes' of vagrants thanks to new printing technology. Over 20% of the rural population were considered 'poor' (i.e. impoverished) and so these fears were easy to feed. Furthermore, as it was up to the local gentry and JPs (Justices of the Peace) to enforce these laws there was a great deal of inconsistency in their application.

As population levels started to rise in the second half of the sixteenth century, pressure on land for food and work increased, and the enclosure of common land, whether agreed amicably among farmers or enforced illegally by greedy landlords, was seen by distressed groups as the cause of their grief. For much of the period grain prices rose ahead of wool prices and enclosure attracted less political attention. By 1590s, however, private profit was replacing communal co-operation. Allegations that common lands had been fenced off, villagers denied rights of pasturage and land converted from arable to pasture lay behind events in Oxfordshire in 1596.

The 'Rising'

The ringleader of the Rising was a carpenter from Hampton Poyle named Bartholomew Steer. Along with a small number of associates, Steer formulated a plan to protest against enclosures after between forty and sixty men visited the county's Lord Lieutenant, Lord Norris, and asked him to help the poor. However the protest soon escalated into a more violent plot, first to throw down the enclosures themselves and then to sieze weapons from the Lord Lieutenant's residence and kill several local landowners. Steer and two brothers, millers James and Richard Bradshaw, tried to recruit further support as they travelled round the local area.

Steer arranged for the plotters to meet on Enslow Hill at 9pm on 21st November, assuming they would attract wide support, and proposed they march to London after attacking local targets in order to link up with the London apprentices. Steer seems to have selected Enslow Hill due to folk memories of a previous rising (centred on resistance to religious reforms) that was suppressed there in 1549: he told one man that the commons had risen and then been "hung like dogs" after being persuaded to return home, but that he intended to go through with his plan. However there were some signs that people were nervous about committing themselves. When Steer asked his brother how much support he could expect in Witney and received a discouraging response, he commented that "*if all men were of that mind they might live like slaves as he did. But for himself happ what would, for he could die but once and [...] he would not alwaies live like a slave*".

Four men gathered at Enslow Hill (Steer, Thomas Horne, a servant, Robert Burton, a mason, and Edward Bompass, a fuller who had promised support from the neighbouring village of Kirtlington), but no one else joined in and they disbanded after two hours. It is possible that they were victims of a misunderstanding, as a larger group of armed men, who remained anonymous, had been seen to gather on the hill the preceding Sunday. It also seems likely that the men's proposal of violent methods and their marginal status in the community as young, landless artisans (Steer and Bompass were both 28, and others involved were of a similar age and status) contributed to the lack of support. The plotters were quickly arrested after a servant, Roger Symonds, informed his landlord of the plan: Burton was taken in London, where he may have been attempting to solicit support among the City apprentices. Although Norris himself tried to play down the significance of the 'Rising', the Privy Council clearly considered this rebellion threatening in the context of the time and the climate of general dissatisfaction. Sir Edward Coke advised that the ringleaders were liable for charges of treason under a 1571 Act, although it appears that not all the statute's legal requirements had in fact been met.

Five principal ringleaders - Steer, James and Richard Bradshaw, Bompass, and Burton were taken to London, interrogated and imprisoned for six months and then sentenced to death for making war against the Queen. Around twenty other men were also imprisoned or interrogated, though not charged with treason. As the authorities were eager to discover if any gentry were involved in the conspiracy, the use of torture was authorised, and Coke pursued the charges with extreme aggression, despite the misgivings of several judges regarding his interpretation of the statutes. Coke appears to have based his arguments on defective knowledge of a riot that took place on May Day 1517, the so called "Evil May Day". Steer in his defiant testimony claimed that he "*stood in no need*" himself, but "*meant to have risen to help his poor friends, and other poor people in misery*".

Despite the charge of treason, on the terms of the 1571 statute, being "shaky" at best, the men were tried before an Oxfordshire jury including several men who had been personally threatened by the plot. Steer and James Bradshaw were both absent from the 24th February arraignment, suggesting they had died in prison in the meantime. Two plotters, Burton and Richard Bradshaw, were convicted and eventually executed on Enslow Hill. The fate of Bompass is unclear, though it is possible he also died in prison. Though the trials themselves and executions passed unrecorded at the time, the convictions for treason of Burton and Bradshaw were used by Coke in the trial of Robert Devereux, 2nd Earl of Essex to support his prosecution. In a more positive outcome of the 'Rising', Parliament subsequently passed an Act halting further enclosures.

Source http://en.wikipedia.org/wiki/ Oxfordshire_Rising_of_1596

Pilgrimage of Grace

Pilgrimage of Grace

A banner bearing the Holy Wounds of Jesus Christ, which was carried at the Pilgrimage of Grace

Location	York, Yorkshire, England
Date	October 1536–February 1537
Attack type	Uprising and subsequent suppression
Perpetrators	Thomas Cromwell, Vicegerent in Spirituals to Henry VIII
	Henry VIII of England
Participant	40,000 pilgrims
Defenders	Robert Aske
	Thomas Darcy, Baron Darcy
	Robert Constable
	Sir Francis Bigod

The **Pilgrimage of Grace** was a popular rising in York, England during 1536, in protest against Henry VIII's break with the Roman Catholic Church and the Dissolution of the Monasteries, as well as other specific political, social and economic grievances. It was done in action against policies initiated by Thomas Cromwell. Technically the term *Pilgrimage of Grace* refers specifically and inclusively to the uprising around York, though sometimes it is used in relation to the risings in general which took place around northern England; first from Lincolnshire, twelve days before the actual *Pilgrimage of Grace*.

Lincolnshire Rising

The **Lincolnshire Rising** was a brief dissent of Roman Catholics against the establishment of the Church of England by Henry VIII and the dissolution of the monasteries set in motion by Thomas Cromwell's suggested plan of asserting the nation's religious autonomy and the king's supremacy over religious matters.

It began at St. James Church, Louth, after evensong on 1 October 1536, shortly after the closure of Louth Abbey. The stated aim of the uprising was only against the attempt to suppress the religious houses, these being Catholic, and was not against Henry VIII himself. It quickly gained support in Horncastle, Market Rasen, Caistor and other nearby towns. Angry with the actions of commissioners, the protesters/rioters demanded the end of the collection of a subsidy, the end of the Ten Articles, an end to the dissolution, an end to taxes in peacetime, a purge of heretics in government, and the repeal of the Statute of Uses. With support from local gentry, a force of demonstrators, estimated at up to 40,000, marched on Lincoln and, by 14 October, occupied Lincoln Cathedral. They demanded the freedom to continue worshipping as

Plaque commemorating the Lincolnshire Rising, opposite south entrance to St James's church, Louth.

Catholics, and protection for the treasures of Lincolnshire churches. It was led by a monk and a shoemaker, and involved 22,000 people.

The moratorium effectively ended on 4 October 1536, when King Henry sent word for the occupiers to disperse or face the forces of Charles Brandon, 1st Duke of Suffolk, which had already been mobilised. By 14 October, few remained in Lincoln. Following the rising, the vicar of Louth and Captain Cobbler, two of the main leaders, were captured and hanged at Tyburn. Most of the other local ringleaders met the same fate over the next twelve days, with a lawyer from Willingham being hanged, drawn and quartered for his involvement. Soon, however, the Lincolnshire Rising helped inspire the more widespread Pilgrimage of Grace.

Pilgrimage of Grace, the early Tudor crisis

Pilgrimage of Grace

The movement broke out on 13 October 1536, immediately following the failure of the Lincolnshire Rising, and only at this point was the term 'Pilgrimage of Grace' used. The causes of the expostulations have long been debated by historians, but several key themes can be identified:

Economic grievances. The northern gentry had concerns over the new Statute of Uses. The harvest of 1535 had also led to high food prices, which may have contributed to discontent.

Political grievances. Many people in

northern England had disliked the way in which Henry VIII had 'cast off' Catherine of Aragon. Although her successor, Anne Boleyn, had been unpopular, both as Catherine's replacement, a rumoured Protestant and a Southerner, her execution in 1536 on trumped-up charges of adultery and treason had done much to undermine the monarchy's prestige and the king's personal reputation. There was also anger at the rise of Thomas Cromwell, who was 'base born', and thus strongly objected to by the aristocracy.

Religious grievances. The local church was, for many in the north, the centre of community life. Many ordinary peasants were worried that their church plate would be confiscated. There were also popular rumours at the time which hinted that baptism might be taxed. The recently-released Ten Articles and the new order of prayer issued by the government in 1535 had also made official doctrine more reformed. This went against the conservative beliefs of most northerners.

Robert Aske was chosen to lead the insurgents; he was a London barrister, a resident of the Inns of Court, and the youngest son of Sir Robert Aske of Aughton near Selby. His was an old Yorkshire family from Richmondshire (Aske Hall). In 1536 Aske led a band of nine thousand followers, who entered and occupied York. There he arranged for the expelled monks and nuns to return to their houses; the king's newly-installed tenants were driven out and Catholic observance resumed. The success of the rising was so great that the royal leaders, Thomas Howard, 3rd Duke of Norfolk and George Talbot, 4th Earl of Shrewsbury, opened negotiations with the insurgents at Scawsby Leys near Doncaster, where Aske had assembled between thirty and forty thousand people.

Henry authorised Norfolk to promise a general pardon and a Parliament to be held at York within a year, as well as a reprieve for the abbeys until the parliament had met. Trusting in the king's promises, Aske dismissed his followers.

Suppression

In February 1537 a new rising took place in Cumberland and Westmorland called Bigod's Rebellion (not authorised by Aske) under Sir Francis Bigod, of Settrington in the North Riding of Yorkshire. Upon this the king arrested Aske and several of the other leaders, such as Lord Darcy, Lord Hussey who was Chief Butler of England, Sir Robert Constable, and Bigod, all of whom were convicted of treason and executed. On March 1537 Thomas Moigne, Member of Parliament for Lincoln was hanged, drawn and quartered. Lords Darcy and Hussey were both beheaded whilst Constable and Bigod were both hanged at Tyburn. Aske was also hanged in chains from the walls of York Castle as a warning to other would-be 'rebels'. In all, 216 were put to death; lords and knights, half a dozen abbots, 38 monks, and 16 parish priests, including :Sir Thomas Percy, Sir Stephen Hamerton, Sir William Lumley, Sir John Constable, Sir William Constable, Adam Sedbar, Abbot of Jervaulx, William Trafford, Abbot of Sawley, Matthew Mackarel, Abbot of Barlings and Bishop of Chalcedon, William Thirsk, Abbot of Fountains and the Prior of Bridlington were all executed and hanged at Tyburn between June and July 1537. Bowbearer of the Forest of Bowland Sir Nicholas Tempast was hanged at Tyburn Sir John Bulmer and his wife Margaret Stafford were also executed, Sir John by being hanged, drawn and quartered whilst his wife was burnt at the stake in Smithfield, London. On November 1538 Keeper of the Sewer Sir Edward Neville was beheaded for his part in the conspiracy. The loss of the leaders enabled the Duke of Norfolk to quell the rising and martial law was imposed upon the demonstrating regions, ending predication.

Successes and failures

The Lincolnshire Rising and the Pilgrimage of Grace have traditionally been seen as complete failures. They did, however, achieve several results that suggest otherwise.

Contrary to popular myth, there were some partial successes because of the rebellions:

The government postponed the collection of the October subsidy. This had been a major grievance amongst the Lincolnshire organisations.

The Statute of Uses was negated by a new law, the Statute of Wills.

Four of the seven sacraments that were omitted from the Ten Articles were restored in the Bishop's Book of 1537. This marked the end of the drift of official doctrine towards Protestantism. The Bishop's Book was followed by the Six Articles of 1539.

An onslaught upon heresy was promised in a royal proclamation in 1538.

Failures

England was not reconciled to the Catholic Church, except during the brief reign of Mary I.

The dissolution of the monasteries continued unabated, with the largest monasteries being dissolved by 1540.

Great tracts of land were seized from the Church and divided among the monarchy and its supporters.

The moves towards official Protestantism achieved by Cromwell were not reversed except during the five-year reign of Mary I (1553–1558).

Source http://en.wikipedia.org/wiki/Pilgrimage_of_Grace

Prayer Book Rebellion

Prayer Book Rebellion		
Date	1549	
Location	Cornwall, Devon	
Result	Victory for Edwardian forces, rebellion suppressed, execution of rebel commanders	
Belligerents		

Southwestern Catholics	Forces of Edward VI
Commanders and leaders	
Sir Humphrey Arundell	Edward Seymour, 1st Duke of Somerset
John Winslade	John Russell, 1st Earl of Bedford
	Anthony Kingston
	William Francis
Strength	
~7,000 rebels	~8,600 troops, including German and Italian mercenaries
Casualties and losses	
At least 2,000 killed	At least 300 killed
Unknown wounded	Unknown wounded
~5,500 deaths	

For the revolts in the 1620s and 30s, see Western Rising

The **Prayer Book Rebellion**, **Prayer Book Revolt**, **Prayer Book Rising**, **Western Rising** or **Western Rebellion** was a popular revolt in Cornwall and Devon, in 1549. In 1549 the Book of Common Prayer, presenting the theology of the English Reformation, was introduced. The change was widely unpopular — particularly in areas of still firmly Catholic religious loyalty (even after the Act of Supremacy in 1534) such as Lancashire. Along with poor economic conditions, the attack on the Church led to an explosion of anger in Devon and Cornwall, initiating an uprising. In response, Edward Seymour, 1st Duke of Somerset, sent Lord John Russell with an army composed partly of German and Italian mercenaries to suppress the revolt.

In June 2007 the Bishop of Truro, the Right Reverend Bill Ind, described the Church of England's role in the massacre of thousands of Catholic rebels during the suppression of the Prayer Book rebellion as an *"enormous mistake"*.

Background

One probable cause of the Prayer Book Rebellion is the religious changes re-

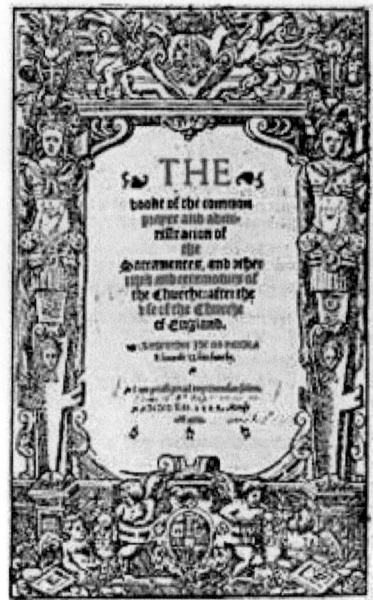
Cranmer's Prayer book of 1549

cently implemented by the government of the new king, Edward VI. In the late 1540s, Lord Protector Somerset, on behalf of the young king, introduced a range of legislative measures as an extension of the Reformation in England and Wales, the primary aim being to change theology and practices of the Church of England along Protestant lines.

In 1549 the Book of Common Prayer, reflecting the theology of Protestantism while keeping much of the appearance of the old rites, replaced, in English, the four old liturgical books in Latin. The change was unpopular, particularly in areas of traditionally Roman Catholic religious loyalty, for example, in Devon and Cornwall.

When traditional religious processions and pilgrimages were banned, commissioners were sent out to remove all symbols of Catholicism, in line with Thomas Cranmer's religious policies favouring Protestantism ever more. In Cornwall, this task was given to William Body, whose perceived desecration of religious shrines led to his murder on 5 April 1548, by William Kylter and Pascoe Trevian at Helston.

This pressure on the lower classes was compounded by the recent poll tax on sheep. This would have affected the region significantly, the West Country being an area of sheep farming. Rumours circulating that the tax would be extended to other livestock may have increased the discontent.

A damaged social structure then meant this local uprising was not sufficiently dealt with by landowners nearby. The Henry Courtenay, 1st Marquess of Exeter, a large landowner in Sampford Courtenay, had recently been attainted. His successor, Lord Russell, was based in London and rarely came out to his land. It is possible this created a lack of local power, who would have normally been expected to quell the revolt.

It is possible that the roots of the rebellion can be traced back to Cornwall's own ancient wish for independence from England, meaning they were loath to accept new laws from a central government geographically distant from them. More recently, the Cornish Rebellion of 1497 and the subsequent destruction of monasteries from 1536 through to 1545 under king Henry VIII which brought an end to the formal scholarship, supported by the monastic orders, that had sustained the Cornish and Devonian cultural identities. The dissolution of Glasney College and Crantock College played a significant part in fomenting opposition to future cultural reforms. It has been argued that the Catholic Church had "proved itself extremely accommodating of Cornish language and culture" and that government attacks on the traditional religion had reawakened the spirit of defiance in Cornwall, and in particular the majority Cornish-speaking far west.

Immediate retribution followed with the execution of twenty-eight Cornishmen at Launceston Castle. One execution of a "traitor of Cornwall" occurred on Plymouth Hoe—town accounts give details of the cost of timber for both gallows and poles. Martin Geoffrey, the pro-Catholic priest of St Keverne, near Helston, was taken to London. After execution, his head was impaled on a staff erected upon London Bridge as was customary.

Sampford Courtenay and the immediate beginnings of the uprising

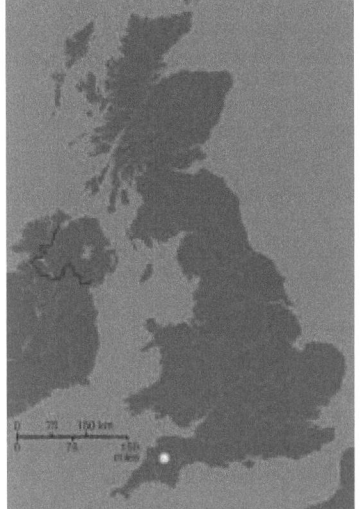

Sampford Courtenay is where the rebellion started, and where the rebels were defeated.

The new prayer book was not uniformly adopted, and in 1549 the Act of Uniformity made it unlawful to use the Latin liturgical rites from Whitsunday 1549 onwards. Magistrates were given the task of enforcing the change. Following the enforced change on Whitsunday, on Whitmonday the parishioners of Sampford Courtenay in Devon compelled their priest to revert to the old service. The rebels argued that the new English liturgy was "but lyke a Christmas game." This claim was probably related to the book's provision for men and women to file into the quire on different sides in order to receive the sacrament, which seemed to remind the Devon men of country dancing. Justices arrived at the next service to enforce the change. An altercation at the service led to a proponent of the change (William Hellyons) being killed by being run through with a pitchfork on the steps of the church house.

Following this confrontation a group of parishioners from Sampford Courtenay decided to march to Exeter to protest at the introduction of the new prayer book. As the group of rebels moved through Devon they gained large numbers of Catholic supporters and became a significant force. Marching east to Crediton, the Devon rebels laid siege to Exeter, demanding the withdrawal of all English liturgies. Although a number of the inhabitants in Exeter sent a message of support to the rebels, the city refused to open its gates. The gates were to stay closed because of the siege for over a month.

"Kill all the gentlemen"

Thomas Cranmer, chief author of the *Book of Common Prayer*.

Edward Seymour, 1st Duke of Somerset, his response was swift and crushing.

Both in Cornwall and Devon, the issue of the Book of Common Prayer seems to have been the straw that broke the camel's back. Two decades of oppression were lately added two years of rampant inflation, in which wheat prices had quadrupled. Along with the rapid enclosure of common lands, the attack on the Church, which was felt to be central to the rural community, led to an explosion of anger. In Cornwall, an army gathered at the town of Bodmin under the leadership of its mayor, Henry Bray, and two staunch Catholic landowners, Sir Humphrey Arundell of Helland and John Winslade of Tregarrick.

Many of the gentry sought protection in old castles. Some shut themselves in St Michael's Mount where they were besieged by the rebels, who started a bewildering smoke-screen by burning trusses of hay. This, combined with a shortage of food and the distress of their women, forced them to surrender. Sir Richard Grenville found refuge in the ruins of Trematon Castle. Deserted by many of his followers, the old man was enticed outside to parley. He was seized and the castle ransacked. Sir Richard and his companions were imprisoned in Launceston gaol. The Cornish army then proceeded to march east across the Tamar border into Devon to join with the Devon rebels near Crediton.

The slogan "Kill all the gentlemen and we will have the Six Articles up again and ceremonies as they were in King Henry's time" highlights the religious aims of the rebellion. However, it also implies a social cause (a view supported by historians such as Guy and Fletcher). That later demands included limiting the size of households belonging to the gentry — theoretically beneficial in a time of population growth and unemployment — possibly suggests an attack on the prestige of the gentry. Certainly such contemporaries as Thomas Cranmer took this view, condemning the rebels for deliberately inciting a class conflict by their demands: "to diminish their strength and to take away their friends, that you might command gentlemen at your pleasures". Protector Somerset himself saw dislike of the gentry as a common factor in all of the 1549 rebellions: "indeed all hath conceived a wonderful hate against the gentlemen and taketh them all as their enemies."

The Cornish rebels were also concerned with the use of the English language in the new prayer book. The language-map of Cornwall at this time is quite complicated, but philological studies have suggested that the Cornish language had been in territorial retreat throughout the Middle Ages. Summarising these researches, Stoyle says that by 1450, the county was divided into three main linguistic blocs: "West Cornwall was inhabited by a population of Celtic descent, which was mostly Cornish speaking; the western part of East Cornwall was inhabited by a population of Celtic descent, which had largely abandoned the Cornish tongue in favor of English; and the eastern part of East Cornwall was inhabited by a population of Anglo-Saxon descent, which was entirely English speaking."

In any case, the West Cornish reacted badly to the introduction of English in the 1549 services. The eighth Article of the *Demands of the Western Rebels* states: "and so we the Cornyshe men (whereof certen of us understande no Englysh) utterly refuse thys newe English". Responding to this, however, Archbishop Cranmer asked why the Cornishmen should be offended by holding the service in English rather than Cornish, when they had before held it in Latin and not understood that.

Confrontations

In London, King Edward VI and his Privy Council became alarmed by this news from the West Country. On instructions from the Lord Protector the Duke of Somerset, one of the Privy Councillors, Sir Gawain Carew, was ordered to *pacify* the rebels. At the same time Lord John Russell was ordered to take an army, including German and Italian mercenaries, and impose a military solution.

The rebels were of many different backgrounds, some farmers, some tin miners, and some fishermen. Cornwall appears to have had a significantly larger militia than other areas of a similar size.

Crediton confrontation

After the rebels passed Plymouth, Devonian knights Sir Gawain and Sir Peter Carew, were sent to negotiate, meeting the Devon rebels at Crediton. They found the approaches blocked and were attacked by longbowmen. Shortly before the Cornish rebels arrived and Arundell now divided his combined force, sending one force to Clyst St Mary to assist the villagers, with the main army advancing upon Exeter, where it besieged the city for 5 weeks.

The Siege of Exeter

The rebel commanders unsuccessfully tried to persuade John Blackaller, Exeter's pro-Catholic mayor, to surrender the town. The city gates were closed as the initial force of some 2,000 gathered outside.

Battle of Fenny Bridges

On 2 July Lord John Russell, 1st Earl of Bedford's initial force had reached Honiton. It included 160 Italian arquebusiers and a thousand landsknechts, German footsoldiers, under the command of Lord William Grey. With promised reinforcements from Wiltshire and Gloucestershire, Russell would have more than 8,600 men, including a cavalry force of 850 men, all of them well armed and well trained. Russell had estimated the combined rebel forces from Cornwall and Devon at only 7,000 men. On 28 July Arundell decided to block their approach to Exeter at Fenny Bridges. The result of this conflict was inconclusive and around 300 on each side were reported to have died with Lord Russell and his army returning to Honiton.

Battle of Woodbury Common

Lord Russell's reinforcements arrived on 2 August and his army of 5000 men began a march upon Exeter, westward, across the downs. Russell's advance continued on to Woodbury Common where they pitched camp. On 4 August the rebels attacked but the result was inconclusive with large numbers of prisoners taken by Lord Russell.

Battle of Clyst St Mary

Arundell's forces re-grouped with the main contingent of 6,000 at Clyst St Mary, but on 5 August were attacked by a central force led by Sir William Francis. After a ferocious battle Russell's troops gained the advantage leaving a thousand Cornish and Devonians dead and many more taken prisoner.

Clyst Heath massacre

Russell pitched camp on Clyst Heath and it was here that 900 bound and gagged prisoners had their throats slit in 10 minutes according to the chronicler John Hayward.

Battle of Clyst Heath

When news of the atrocity reached Arundell's forces a new attack took place early on 6 August. Lord Grey was later to comment that he had never seen the like, nor taken part in such a murderous fray. As he had led the charge against the Scots in the Battle of Pinkie Cleugh, this was a telling statement. Some 2000 died at the battle of Clyst Heath. A group of Devon men went north up the valley of the Exe, where they were overtaken by Sir Gawen Carew, who left the corpses of their leaders hanging on gibbets from Dunster to Bath.

Relief of Exeter

Lord Russell continued his attack with the relief of Exeter. In London, a proclamation was issued allowing the lands of those involved in the uprising to be confiscated. Arundell's estates were transferred to Sir Gawen Carew and Sir Peter Carew was rewarded with all of John Wynslade's Devon estates.

Battle of Sampford Courtenay

Lord Russell was under the impression that the Cornish had been defeated but news arrived that Arundell's army was re-grouping at Sampford Courtenay. This interrupted his plans to send 1,000 men into Cornwall by ship to cut off his enemy's retreat. Russell's forces were strengthened by the arrival of a force under Provost Marshal Sir Anthony Kingston. His army now numbered more than 8,000, vastly outnumbering what remained of his opposition. Lord Grey and Sir William Herbert led the attack and contemporary Exeter historian John Hooker wrote that 'the Cornish would not give in until most of their number had been slain or captured.' Lord John Russell, reported that his army had killed between five and six hundred and his pursuit of the Cornish retreat killed a further seven hundred.

Aftermath

Many escaped including Arundell, who fled to Launceston. There he was later to be captured and taken to London with Wynslade, who was caught at Bodmin. In total over 5,500 people lost their lives in the rebellion. Further orders were issued on behalf of the king by the Lord Protector the Duke of Somerset, and Archbishop Thomas Cranmer for the continuance of the onslaught. Under Sir Anthony Kingston, English and mercenary forces then moved throughout Devon and into Cornwall and executed or killed many people before the bloodshed finally ceased. Proposals to translate the Prayer Book into Cornish were also suppressed.

The loss of life in the prayer book rebellion and subsequent reprisals as well

Penryn, Prayer Book Rebellion Memorial, near the site of Glasney College.

as the introduction of the English prayer book is seen as a turning point in the Cornish language, for which — unlike Welsh — a complete bible translation was not produced. Research has also suggested that prior to the rebellion the Cornish language had strengthened and more concessions had been made to Cornwall as a "nation", and that anti-English sentiment had been growing stronger, providing additional impetus for the rebellion.

Bishop of Truro expresses regret for the brutal response to the Prayer Book Rebellion

In June 2007 the then Bishop of Truro, The Rt Revd Bill Ind, was reported as saying that the massacre during the vicious suppression of the Cornish Prayerbook rebellion more than 450 years ago was an "enormous mistake" for which the Church of England should be ashamed. Speaking at a ceremony at Pelynt, he said:

"I am often asked about my attitude to the Prayerbook Rebellion and in my opinion, there is no doubt that the English Government behaved brutally and stupidly and killed many Cornish people. I don't think apologising for something that happened over 500 years ago helps, but I am sorry about what happened and I think it was an enormous mistake."

Source http://en.wikipedia.org/wiki/Prayer_Book_Rebellion

Ridolfi plot

The Ridolfi plot was meant to put Mary Stuart on the throne of England.

The **Ridolfi plot** was a plot in 1571 to assassinate Queen Elizabeth I of England and replace her with Mary, Queen of Scots. The plot was hatched and planned by Roberto di Ridolfi, an international banker who was able to travel between Brussels, Rome and Madrid to gather support without attracting too much suspicion.

Background

The Duke of Norfolk, a cousin to the Queen and the wealthiest landowner in the country, had been proposed as a possible husband for Mary since her imprisonment in 1568. This suited Norfolk, who had ambitions and felt Elizabeth persistently undervalued him. In pursuit of his goals, he agreed to support the Northern Rebellion, though he quickly lost his nerve and tried to call it off. As the rebellion was not under his control, it progressed, with the Northern earls trying to foment rebellion among their Catholic subjects to prepare for a Catholic Spanish invasion by the Duke of Alba, governor of the Netherlands.

After the rebellion failed, the leaders were executed and a purge of Catholic sympathisers in the priesthood carried out. Norfolk was imprisoned in the Tower of London for nine months and only freed under house arrest when he confessed all and begged for mercy. Pope Pius V issued *Regnans in Excelsis*, a papal bull excommunicating Elizabeth, shortly afterward, which commanded all faithful Catholics to do all they could to depose her. The majority of English Catholics ignored the bull. In response, Elizabeth became much harsher to Catholics and their sympathisers.

Plot

Roberto Ridolfi, a Florentine banker and ardent Catholic, had been involved in the planning of the Northern rebellion, and had been plotting to overthrow Elizabeth as early as 1569. With the failure of the rebellion, he concluded that foreign intervention was needed to restore Catholicism and bring Mary to the English throne, and began to contact potential conspirators. Mary's advisor, John Lesley, the Bishop of Ross, gave his assent to the plot as the way to free Mary. The plan was to have the Duke of Alba invade from the Netherlands with 10,000 men, foment a rebellion of the northern English nobility, murder Elizabeth, and marry Mary to Thomas Howard, 4th Duke of Norfolk. Ridolfi optimistically estimated half of all English peers were Catholic, and could muster in excess of 39,000 men. Norfolk gave verbal assurances to Ridolfi that he was Catholic, though as a pupil of John Foxe, he remained a Protestant all his life. Both Mary and Norfolk, desperate to remedy their respective situations, agreed to the plot. With their blessing, Ridolfi set off to the Continent to gain Alba, Pius V and King Philip II's support.

While desiring the restoration of Catholic rule in England, the Duke of Alba feared the accession of Mary, Queen of Scots, to the throne of England. As her mother was a member of the prominent Guise family in France, he feared the alliance of England and France by Mary.

Discovery

In 1571, Elizabeth's intelligence network was sending her information about a plot against her life. By gaining the confidence of Spain's ambassador to England, John Hawkins learned the details of the conspiracy and notified the government so to arrest the plotters. She was also sent a private warning by the Grand Duke of Tuscany, who had learned of the plot against her. Charles Baillie, Ridolfi's messenger, was arrested at Dover for carrying compromising letters, and under torture revealed the plot. The Duke of Norfolk was arrested on 7 September 1571 and sent to the Tower. Guerau de Spes, the Spanish ambassador, was expelled from the country in January 1571. Still abroad when the plot was discovered, Ridolfi never returned to England; he became a Florentine senator in 1600.

Mary, when questioned, admitted to having dealings with Ridolfi, but denied any involvement with the plot. Though she was clearly implicated by the evidence, Elizabeth refused to have her executed and vetoed a bill by Parliament that condemned Mary and removed her from the succession. She feared that by executing a "divinely appointed" monarch, she undermined her own position. She proceeded with the execution of the Duke of Norfolk for treason on 2 June 1572. Mary's status in England was transformed from honoured guest to treasonous pariah, and she was universally condemned by the governing elite. Her continued conspiring, especially in the Babington Plot, eventually led to her conviction for treason and execution on 8 February 1587.

Media representations

The Ridolfi Plot was covered in *Mary Queen of Scots* (1971), starring Vanessa Redgrave as Mary and Glenda Jackson as Elizabeth.

An altered and fictionalised version of the Ridolfi Plot was featured in the 1998 film *Elizabeth*, starring Cate Blanchett as Elizabeth. Christopher Eccleston played Thomas Howard, Duke of Norfolk as the chief conspirator and the film omitted the involvement of Ridolfi. In the film the conspiracy included Bishop Stephen Gardiner, a counter-reformer who had died in 1555 before Elizabeth's accession, and John Ballard, who was involved in the later Babington Plot.

Source http://en.wikipedia.org/wiki/Ridolfi_plot

Rising of the North

Rising of the North
Date November 1569 - January 1570
Location Northern England
Result Victory for the Elizabethan forces, strengthening Elizabeth's authority, weakening the aristocracy of the North.

Belligerents

Partisans of Mary, Queen of Scots

Elizabeth I of England

English and Welsh Catholics

English and Welsh Protestants

Scottish Protestants

Commanders and leaders

Earl of Westmorland

Earl of Northumberland

Countess of Westmorland

Aftermath:

Leonard Dacre

Strength

Earl of Sussex

Baron Clinton

Earl of Warwick

Aftermath:

Baron Hunsdon

4,600   7,000

The **Rising of the North** of 1569, also called the **Revolt of the Northern Earls** or **Northern Rebellion**, was an unsuccessful attempt by Catholic nobles from Northern England to depose Queen Elizabeth I of England and replace her with Mary, Queen of Scots

Background

When Elizabeth I succeeded her sister Mary as Queen of England in 1558, her accession was disputed due to the disputed legitimacy of the marriage of the Queen's parents - Henry VIII and Anne Boleyn. Opponents of Elizabeth turned to Mary, Queen of Scots, as the descendant of Henry's sister Margaret Tudor. The claims were initially put forward by Mary's father-in-law, King Henry II of France, but Mary upheld them after her return to Scotland in 1561.

Many English Catholics, then a significant portion of the population, increasingly supported Mary's claim as a means of relief for their situation of religious persecution. This position was especially strong in Northern England, where several powerful nobles were Catholics; there had been similar risings against Henry VIII; the Pilgrimage of Grace of 1536 and Bigod's Rebellion of 1537. Supporters of Mary hoped for aid from France and possibly Spain. Mary's position was strengthened by the birth of her son, James, in 1566 but weakened again when she was deposed in July 1567.

Rebellion under Northumberland and Westmorland

The rebellion was led by Charles Neville, 6th Earl of Westmorland and Thomas Percy, 7th Earl of Northumberland, who in November 1569 occupied Durham and celebrated Mass, in Durham Cathedral. Such public Catholic worship had been prohibited by the Protestant Queen Elizabeth. Westmorland's wife, Jane Howard, played an active part in the rebellion, hoping to arrange a marriage between her brother Thomas Howard, 4th Duke of Norfolk and the prospective Queen Mary.

From Durham, the rebels marched south to Bramham Moor, while Elizabeth struggled to raise forces sufficient to confront them. But, hearing of a large force being raised by the Earl of Sussex, the rebels abandoned plans to besiege York, and captured Barnard Castle instead. They proceeded to Clifford Moor, but found little popular support. Sussex marched out from York on 13 December 1569 with 7,000 men against the rebels' 4,600, and was followed by 12,000 men under Baron Clinton. The rebel earls retreated northward and finally dispersed their forces, fleeing into Scotland.

Leonard Dacre's resistance

A questionable role in the rebellion was played by Leonard Dacre, an early sympathizer of Mary. At the outbreak of the rebellion, he travelled to Elizabeth's court at Windsor to claim the heritage of his young nephew, the 5th Baron Dacre. After the latter's untimely death in 1569, this had descended to his sisters, all married to sons of the Duke of Norfolk. Dacre returned to Northern England, ostensibly a faithful partisan of Elizabeth, but his intentions remain unclear.

After the retreat of the rebels, he seized Greystoke Castle and fortified his own Naworth Castle, where he gathered 3,000 Cumbrian troops and tried to keep up the appearance of good relations with the Queen. He held out against a siege of the royal army under Baron Hunsdon but then attacked the retreating army at Gelt River. Though Hunsdon was outnumbered, he charged Dacre's foot with his cavalry, killing 300-400 and capturing 200-300 men. Dacre escaped via Scotland to Flanders, where he died in exile.

Reprisals

Of the rebellion's leaders, the Earls of Northumberland and Westmorland had fled into Scotland. Northumberland was captured by the Earl of Morton and turned over to Elizabeth in 1572, who had him beheaded at York. After having been hidden at Ferniehirst Castle, Westmorland escaped to Flanders, where he died impoverished. His family lost their ancestral homes and his wife, Jane Howard, also fled to the Continent. She lived the rest of her life under house arrest. Her brother, the Duke of Norfolk, was first imprisoned, then pardoned. He was imprisoned again following the Ridolfi Plot in 1570 and finally executed in 1572. Norfolk's treason charges included "comforting and relieving of the English rebels that stirred the Rebellion in the North since they have fled out of the realm." Altogether, 600 supporters of Mary were executed, while many others fled into exile.

Pope Pius V had tried to aid the rebellion by excommunicating Elizabeth and declaring her deposed in the bull *Regnans in Excelsis*, but the document did not arrive until the rebellion had been suppressed. The bull gave Elizabeth more reason to view Catholics with suspicion. It inspired conspiracies to assassinate her, starting with the Ridolfi plot. In 1587, Elizabeth brought Mary, Queen of Scots to trial for treason; she was convicted by the court and executed. The Spanish used the execution of an anointed queen as the rationale for their attempted invasion by the Spanish Armada the following year.

Source http://en.wikipedia.org/wiki/Rising_of_the_North

Second Cornish Uprising of 1497

The **Second Cornish Uprising** is the name given to the Cornish uprising of September 1497 when the pretender to the throne Perkin Warbeck landed at Whitesand Bay, near Land's End, on 7 September with just 120 men in two ships. Warbeck had seen the potential of the Cornish unrest in the 1st Cornish Rebellion of 1497 even though the Cornish had been defeated at the Battle of Blackheath on 17 June 1497. Warbeck proclaimed that he would put a stop to extortionate taxes levied to help fight a war against Scotland and was warmly welcomed in Cornwall. His wife, Lady Katharine, was left in the safety of St Michael's Mount and when he decided to attack Exeter his supporters declared him 'Richard IV' on Bodmin Moor. Most of the Cornish gentry supported Warbeck's cause after their setback previously in June of that year and on 17 September a Cornish army some 6,000 strong entered Exeter before advancing on Taunton.

Henry VII sent his chief general, Giles, Lord Daubeney, to attack the

Cornish and when Warbeck heard that the King's scouts were at Glastonbury he panicked and deserted his army. Warbeck was captured at Beaulieu Abbey in Hampshire, where he surrendered. Henry VII reached Taunton on 4 October 1497, where he received the surrender of the remaining Cornish army. The ringleaders were executed and others fined an enormous total of £13,000. 'King Richard' was imprisoned, first, at Taunton, then in London, where he was 'paraded through the streets on horseback amid much hooting and derision of the citizens'. On 23 November 1499 Warbeck was drawn on a hurdle from the Tower to Tyburn, London, where he read out a 'confession' and was hanged.

Source http://en.wikipedia.org/wiki/Second_Cornish_Uprising_of_1497

Stafford and Lovell Rebellion

The **Stafford and Lovell rebellion** was the first armed uprising against Henry VII after he won the crown at the Battle of Bosworth in 1485. The uprising was led by Francis Lovell, 1st Viscount Lovell and the Stafford brothers, Sir Humphrey Stafford (c.1426/7 – 8 July 1486) of Grafton, Worcestershire, and Thomas Stafford, and occurred during Eastertime 1486.

Rebellion

The conspirators hoped to restore the Yorkist monarchy. However, the uprising was a disaster. On 22 April 1486 Lord Lovell decided not to risk open rebellion, and escaped to Burgundy. In the meantime the Stafford brothers had risen in rebellion in Worcester, despite the fact that King Henry had mass support in that area.

During this time Henry was in York on a nationwide tour of the country. As soon as he advanced towards Worcester in order to eliminate Yorkist support, on 11 May 1586 the Stafford brothers again fled to sanctuary, this time at Culham.

Consequences

The King took immediate action. Stafford was forcibly removed from sanctuary on the night of 13 May by John Savage and sixty followers. Henry then ordered the execution of Humphrey Stafford of Grafton, but pardoned the younger Thomas Stafford.

The arrest prompted a series of protests to Pope Innocent VIII over the breaking of sanctuary; these resulted in a Papal bull in August which severely limited the rights of sanctuary, excluding it completely in cases of treason, thereby vindicating the King's actions.

Source http://en.wikipedia.org/wiki/Stafford_and_Lovell_Rebellion

The Earl of Essex Rebellion

The Earl of Essex

Essex's Rebellion was an unsuccessful rebellion led by Robert Devereux, 2nd Earl of Essex in 1601 against Elizabeth I of England and the court faction led by Sir Robert Cecil to gain further influence at court.

Rebellion

The rebellion took place in 1601. In August of that year Essex was granted his freedom, but the source of his basic income—the sweet wines monopoly—was not renewed. His situation had become desperate, and he shifted "from sorrow and repentance to rage and rebellion." In early 1601, he began to fortify Essex House, his town mansion on the Strand, and gathered his followers. On the morning of 8 February, he marched out of Essex House with a party of nobles and gentlemen (some later involved in the 1605 Gunpowder Plot) and entered the city of London in an attempt to force an audience with the Queen. Cecil immediately had him proclaimed a traitor. A force under Sir John Leveson placed a barrier across the street at Ludgate Hill. When Essex's men tried to force their way through, Essex's stepfather, Sir Christopher Blount, was injured in the resulting skirmish, and Essex withdrew with his men to Essex House. Essex surrendered after Crown forces besieged Essex House.

Aftermath

Within ten days Essex was condemned for treason and within another week was beheaded.

Source http://en.wikipedia.org/wiki/The_Earl_of_Essex_Rebellion

Wyatt's rebellion

Wyatt's Rebellion was a popular uprising in England in 1554, named after Thomas Wyatt, one of its leaders. The

Portrait of Thomas Wyatt the Younger by Hans Holbein the Younger, circa 1540-42

rebellion arose out of concern over Queen Mary I's determination to marry Philip II of Spain, which was an unpopular policy with the English. Queen Mary's overthrow was implied in the rebellion, although not expressly stated as a goal.

Motives

The precise reason for the uprisings has been subject to much debate. Many historians, such as D.M. Loades, consider the rebellion to have been primarily motivated by political considerations, not easily separated from religious ones in the 16th century, and notably the desire to prevent the unpopular marriage of Queen Mary to Prince Philip of Spain. On 16 November 1553 a Parliamentary delegation had waited upon Queen Mary, and formally requested that she choose an English husband, the obvious though tacit candidate being her kinsman Edward Courtenay, recently created Earl of Devon. The rebels explained that the reason for the rebellion was "to prevent us from over-running by strangers." Nevertheless, all the rebel leaders were committed Protestants.

Initial plans

There were four chief rebel leaders:
Sir Thomas Wyatt, who owned large areas of land in Kent and had great influence there
Sir James Croft, who came from an influential Herefordshire family
Sir Peter Carew, who was an MP for Devon
Henry Grey, 1st Duke of Suffolk, who was based in Leicestershire.

Other rebels, aside from Edward Courtenay, Earl of Devon, included Sir Henry Isley, Lord John Grey of Wilton, Lord Thomas Grey (Henry Grey's brother), Sir William Thomas (Clerk of the Privy Council), Sir Nicholas Throckmorton, John Harington, 1st Baron Harington of Exton, Sir Nicholas Arnold and Sir William St Loe. Others involved included the French ambassador, Antoine de Noailles, who knew that a Spanish king on the throne of England was not in the best interests of France, and the mathematician Leonard Digges.

Each of the four leaders would raise rebellions in one of the four counties, and together they would converge on London, on 18 March 1554. They would then replace Mary with her half-sister Elizabeth, who would then marry Lord Devon. Meanwhile, a fleet of French ships would prevent Philip of Spain from reaching England.

Implementation of these plans was prevented when Simon Renard, the Imperial ambassador to England, suspected a plot. He informed the Lord Chancellor, Bishop Stephen Gardiner, who on 21 January arrested Devon, who revealed that there was indeed a rebellion planned. Under increased pressure of time, the planned rebellion was moved forward and went awry.

The following day Sir James Croft delivered a message to Elizabeth at Ashridge House in Hertfordshire, but realizing that under the circumstances a rebellion would be unsafe, Croft gave up. Grey proved more determined, but only managed to raise a force of 140 rebels, many of whom were his own men. He was refused entry to Coventry, and gave himself up. He was later tried and beheaded, as were his daughter Lady Jane Grey, and her husband Lord Guilford Dudley, both still in prison since the failed attempt to put Lady Jane on the throne and neither of whom were involved in the uprising.

News that Sir Peter Carew was spreading dissent at Exeter in Devon by saying publicly that a Spanish king would bring the Spanish Inquisition reached the Court in January 1554. Carew attempted to raise support for the uprising in Devon, but the Protestant nobles there proved unwilling to commit treason, and the county's peasant inhabitants were largely Catholic. Also, he had played a large part in crushing the earlier Prayer Book Rebellion there. A warrant was issued for Carew's arrest, but, forewarned, he escaped across the Channel to Normandy, but was arrested soon after. By this time, the French ships found themselves unable to maintain their position and returned to France.

Only Wyatt succeeded in raising a substantial force. On 22 January 1554 he summoned a meeting of his friends at his castle of Allington, and 25 January was now fixed for the rising.

Rebellion

On 26 January Wyatt occupied Rochester, and issued a proclamation to the county. Many country people and local gentry collected. At first the queen's supporters, led by Lord Abergavenny and Sir Robert Southwell, the sheriff, appeared to be able to suppress the rising with ease, routing a rebel force of 500 at Hartley Wood on 28 January. But the Spanish marriage was unpopular, and Kent was more affected by the preaching of the reformers than most of the country districts of England. Abergavenny and Southwell were deserted by their men, who either disbanded or went over to Wyatt. He now had 3,000 men at his command. A detachment of the London trainbands was sent against him under the command of the elderly Duke of Norfolk. But they also joined the rebels, raising their numbers to 4,000, while the Duke fled to London.

Elizabeth, meanwhile, had been summoned to Court and was held incommunicado, in mortal fear for her life. The rising now seemed so formidable that the queen and council sent a deputation to Wyatt to ask for his terms.

He demanded that the Tower of London should be surrendered to him, and the queen put under his charge. The insolence of these demands turned an initially sympathetic London against Wyatt, and Mary was able to rally the capital to her cause on 1 February by delivering a rousing speech at the Guildhall.

Wyatt's army reached Southwark on 3 February. Mary's supporters occupied London Bridge in force, and the rebels were unable to penetrate into the city. Wyatt was driven from Southwark by the threats of Sir John Brydges, afterwards Lord Chandos, who was prepared to fire on the suburb with the guns of the Tower.

Refusing to give up, the rebels marched to Kingston. The bridge there was also destroyed, but the rebels repaired it and crossed over. They met little resistance as they marched through the outskirts of London, but were stopped by the inhabitants of Ludgate. The rebel army then broke up.

Aftermath

Wyatt surrendered, and was tried and executed along with approximately 90 rebels, many of whom were hanged, drawn and quartered. Wyatt himself, after being severely tortured in the hope of extracting a confession implicating Elizabeth, was beheaded at Tower Hill and his body quartered. Courtenay was exiled and eventually died in Padua. Lord Thomas Grey and William Thomas were both executed. Throckmorton was found not guilty and released. Sir Nicholas Arnold, together with a few other ringleaders, was never brought to trial and eventually pardoned. Sir Peter Carew was imprisoned but released and Sir James Croft was tried and found guilty, but eventually pardoned. William St Loe also evaded punishment.

Elizabeth was intensely interrogated and in danger of execution, but managed to be spared due to evasive and intelligent responses, in which she maintained she had been unaware of the planned uprising. Nothing could be proved, but the degree to which she was privy to the preparations has been questioned by modern scholars. Elizabeth remained imprisoned as a precautionary measure.

The rebellion proved disastrous for the Wyatt family, as they lost their title and lands, including the family home, Allington Castle. However, when Elizabeth, herself a Protestant and distant relative of the Wyatt family, ascended the throne in 1558, she restored the family titles and lands.

Source http://en.wikipedia.org/wiki/Wyatt's_rebellion